A NEW MYTH
FOR AMERICA

by

James Hilgendorf

Library of Congress Control Number 2012933042

ISBN: 978-1-929159-28-4

Published by The Tribute Series
1401 Liberty Street #11
El Cerrito, CA. 94530
(510) 501-9564
www.tributeseries.com

Cover photograph by Andrew Dunn
Website: www.andrewdunnphoto.com
Creative Commons Attribution-Share Alike
2.0 Generic License

CONTENTS

A NEW MYTH FOR AMERICA

THE DREAM OF AMERICA

Every great civilization has had its own myth, a cosmic story of how we fit into the universe, a divine story of who we are and where we came from.

Greece had Chaos and Chronos, Zeus, Athena and Hercules and a pantheon of other gods. Rome had Aeneas and Romulus and Remus. Western civilization had the Old Testament prophets and stories of the Bible.

Now, though many in the world still hang on, these myths are either crumbling or gone to dust.

In the popular television series, "The Power of Myth", in which Bill Moyers interviews Joseph Campbell, one of the foremost authorities on mythology, the following dialogue takes place:

Moyers:

"You've seen what happens when primitive societies are unsettled by white man's civilization. They go to pieces, they disintegrate, they become diseased. Hasn't the same thing been happening to us since our myths began to disappear?"

Campbell:

"Absolutely, it has."

1

Moyers:

"Isn't that why conservative religions today are calling for the old-time religion?"

Campbell:

"Yes, and they're making a terrible mistake. They are going back to something that is vestigial, that doesn't serve life. The old-time religion belongs to another age, another people, another set of human values, another universe. By going back you throw yourself out of sync with history. Our kids lose their faith in the religions that were taught to them, and they go inside."

Moyers:

"Often with the help of a drug."

What we crave is a new consciousness, a new time, new stories, new heroes and heroines, dragons and great knights upon black steeds, the battle, the quest - a story that encompasses the heavens and suns and stars and galaxies and black holes and universes beyond number, yet is bolted down to rocks and rivers and flowers and thunder and rain, finding its tale reverberating through the bones and marrow and hearts of the blacksmith, the nanny, the insurance salesman, the ice cream vendor, the teacher, banker, garbage collector, shoe repairman, mechanic, musician, swelling the chorus of a billion, trillion, quintillion, quadrillion voices of stifled dreams out of the very heart of the universe itself, dreams waiting and unfulfilled, dreams blighted and blasted by war, famine, pestilence, lack of opportunity, oppression - not just any dreams, not just the dreams of a satisfied self, but the dreams of something greater, of justice, love, recognition, and a place in the universe of forever.

The real, true dream and myth of America.

Yes, America.

For the Dream of America has always been a dream that resonated within the minds and hearts of men and women and children around the globe - that shining vision, that dreamt-of and promised land that was almost on another plane of reality. It was a new beginning, a new province of heretofore unfulfilled possibilities for the human race.

We talk of the Dream of America, and consider it originated with the Pilgrim fathers landing upon our shores, the vision of a shining City upon a Hill (even though the City they built - themselves having fled persecution and suffered persecution themselves - was turned into a bastion of intolerance and authoritarianism that drove those who did not fit the mold of the City to seek freedom and salvation elsewhere); or with the Declaration of Independence and its strains of Life, Liberty and the Pursuit of Happiness (even though the signers of this great document and ideals expressed there upheld in their own lives the degradation of slavery - no less a man than one of our own Christian forefathers, Thomas Jefferson, personally held hundreds of slaves in his monied accounts - this same Thomas Jefferson who in 1814 wrote: "...the amalgamation of whites with blacks produces a degradation to which no lover of his country, no lover of excellence in the human character, can innocently consent").

Yes, these are also strains of the American Dream.

In 1864, President Abraham Lincoln, in a letter to Colonel William F. Elkins near the end of the Civil War, wrote:

"We may congratulate ourselves that this cruel war is nearing its end. It has cost a vast amount of treasure and blood...It has indeed been a trying hour for the Republic; but I see in the near future a crisis approaching that unnerves me and causes me to tremble for the safety of my country. As a result of the war, corporations have been enthroned and an era of corruption in high places will follow, and the money power of the country will endeavor to prolong its reign by working upon the prejudices of the people until all wealth is aggregated in a few hands and the Republic is destroyed. i feel at this moment more anxiety for the safety of my country than ever before, even in the midst of war."

He was speaking, of course, of the usurping of economic and political power by the corporations.

This malaise has finally engulfed us.

It is the fruition of what has gone before, the fruit of our false dreams.j

Wars, Afghanistan, Irag, trillions of dollars, devastating our economy, destroying the future of our youth, enriching the coffers of munitions manufacturers, builders of atomic and hydrogen bombs, helicopters, tanks, automatic rifles, armored personnel carriers, perpetual war, supported by a war economy, planes and submarines that die or rot and millions and billions of dollars die or rot with them, to be manufactured all over again, the enormity of the crime of corroding our future for dollars, for greed, all in the name of patriotism, love of country, love of the flag, love of America, and meanwhile our elected leaders glide down the hallowed halls of Congress, wearing bow ties and sharp suits, symbols of greatness and honor, old men who should be cast upon the trash trucks of history, the youth of our country cheated, sent off to war, disemboweled, shorn of life and limb, limping back to a country that is now foreign to them, unrecognized, given short shrift, young men and women coming from fathers and mothers struggling to survive, wondering and praying that their children become greater than they ever were, to find their children shackled by debt, indebted to banks and finance centers, the universities themselves loading up, piling up debt on their shoulders and backs, and the wars go on, and our government does less and less, beholden to money, paid for by money, sold down the river by money, barely anyone with a vision of the people, oh say can you see by the dawn's early light an America desecrated and usurped by leaders mouthing platitudes, what is a leader anyway, a true leader should be sweating and racking brain and soul and body to serve the people, to honor the people, to do everything in one's power to bring happiness to man and woman and child, and meanwhile the tanks and armor and stealth fighters keep regurgitating from factories, chalk up a million dollars apiece, ship them out, man them with our best, send them down the dusty roads to death, blow them up, build more, ten thousand nuclear bombs each one a thousand times greater than the bomb of Hiroshima, it's not enough, build more, update our arsenals, we may need them to wipe out the bastards so that

4

the lone suicide bomber never reaches our beaches or sky-scrapers or tunnels or subways or rivers, blow up all the god-damn countries that think a little different than us, dress different, speak different, worship different, all the devils opposed to our God, to our sanctimonious way of life, our America, America, O beautiful for spacious skies, for amber waves of grain, sing it out everyone, sing the golden tune, America! America! May God thy gold refine, till all success be nobleness, and every gain divine, trillions swept under the rug, derivatives, securitization, swaps, snake oil brokers, snake oil companies, mortgages, trillions and trillions, but pay them back, protect them, save our financial system, save the money, save the crooks, save good old America, God bless America, and down in the streets, the real streets, young men are shooting each other in the dark, and their motto is screw America, the old white America, and they are dying of no jobs and no money but mostly a loss of hope, loss of belief in the good old red white and blue, and of someone who really cares, who will roll up the sleeves and get to work down in the trenches, caring nothing for themselves, but caring for the people, for the youth of this land, for the future.

We are caught now in the drift down. We have not seen the bottom, and a great many revelations are to come.

There is no going back, and all the high-tech world and computers will not save us from the confrontation with ourselves.

It is amid all of this that a new America is struggling to be reborn.

Out of the struggle, out of the pain, out of the creaking dying old structures, new voices, new ways of being, new orbits around our sun, fresh faces of people will emerge.

Writing a new story of the cosmos, the revelation and revolution that has been waiting in the wings since the first dawn of the first sun of time.

A great myth comes forth, bringing forth light and thunder upon a newly birthing world.

5

It is the reason for the existence of the universe itself.

It is one person coming to fruition and bloom.

_____

MEMORIES

I was a young boy, sitting with my father on the back stairs of our house, after I had mown the grass, and he looked down at me and smiled.

The smell of the new mown grass was lovely.

We sat there, no words spoken.

These memories come back, crowding out others, his life with its feeling of loss, the sense of defeat he felt, years succeeding one another with no vision, no purpose finally other than the life of his son sitting there, my father's hopes and dreams all gone, buried by a false American Dream.

How can I ever repay him?

To endure, to endure for another, to hang on beyond hope, the heart threadbare, for the sake of another.

This is the story of humanity.

We were living a dream that had died, though we did not know it. We were walking through ruins and shades and shadows.

My father woke very early every morning, had his coffee, then walked the long lonely quiet back road to the factory, where he tied his body and soul to a heartless machine for the day, while the sun was shining, the birds singing, and all over America machines were working through the day and the night, cauldrons of fire and steel and molten metal gone to cars and tanks and airplanes and bombs bringing a message of progress and happiness to a jubilant world.

The old dreams were crashing, not just for my father, but for the world at large. We moved through the devastation, realizing nothing, because there was nothing to realize, nothing hung together anymore, we were not aware that the buildings and cathedrals of our minds had crumbled to dust, and everything around - the faces of people, businesses, life and death itself - was not the same anymore, there was no more glory, it was all just a fact, nothing more.

What could we do, but look at each other, and remember?

To somehow repay. To foster a true Dream.

This is what my father gave me.

I remember, always.

_____

I WAS THERE FROM THE BEGINNING

I was there from the beginning.

I lived in caves, I fled the darkness, dread serpents, beasts, and the ball of light rose out of mists, again and again, like a god, spears of light breaking over mountains, I found my way once again. And then blackness and night once again, the cold, the quaking, the sound of beasts.

My heart beat with it all. I was there from the beginning.

It was another world. It went on and on, glacial slow, time sloughing through the aeons, no purpose, no eye, just replicating in the dark, and the red glow of suns setting, and nothing again, the death.

I moved through it all. I was there. It was my life. Creation and creation, and urge and urge, the urge to awaken from the dream.

It was all a merging, myself and the liquid black skies, the balls of light, the trees and animals whose blood ran red and hot from the heart of the dark, from the caverns below the earth, from the place we came from, where the animals came from, the place they returned to, the dark, the death again.

My hand was the mover of everything. I placed my hand on the walls of the deep dark caverns. I held my place. I was there with the animals and the dark.

I could feel the dark and the skies singing with great birds.

I was there.

I was there from the beginning.

_____

LIBERATION

"There are those who will say that the liberation of humanity, the freedom of man and mind is nothing but a dream. They are right. It is the American Dream.

-- Archibald MacLeish.

A LOOK INTO THE MIRROR

America is the promise of the self.

It is the unfolding, finally, of everything that was imagined or dreamed.

It is finding the very core of the universe, and all the gods and demons and stars and suns and galaxies, within one's very own heart.

Look into the mirror. Who is there?

Ultra powerful reflector telescopes gather upon smooth polished mirrors ever and ever deeper glimpses into the life of a universe beyond comprehension, gazing back billions of light years into the past. We look into those mirrors, but fail to see ourselves. These images are our own life.

Everything swings on this moment, all time and all space.

America is here and now. There are no fantasy lands here.

Rocks and country roads, skyscrapers, rivers, flowers and fields, they are all right here. We live on this Earth, nowhere else.

All those who have died, from the beginning of time, crowd in upon this land, this America, hovering among the shadows in anticipation, for a word of what is coming, of what is to be revealed.

America is something never before imagined.

THE TREASURE TOWER

They assembled on the mountain, summoned from all parts of the universe, of universes beyond universes, billions and trillions in their retinues, the kings and queens of life, even animals, serpents, devils and demons, and all of them magnificent, come to hear the Buddha expound the Law, the essence of all his teachings, the Lotus Sutra.

A great Treasure Tower, half as large as the earth itself, brilliant with jewels, rose into the air, carrying with it all these innumerable beings, and the Buddha began to expound the Law.

He revealed that, contrary to what everyone believed - that he had first attained enlightenment in his present lifetime while meditating under a bodhi tree - he had, in fact, attained enlightenment in the unimaginably remote past, and had ever since then been in the world preaching the Law. The life of the Buddha is eternal. The universe itself is eternal. Our lives are eternal.

The Treasure Tower and the assembled beings of all the worlds is the Buddha's life itself, a metaphor, a story, a myth of eternity that resides not only in the Buddha's heart and mind, but in the life of each and every human being past, present and future on the face of the planet.

It is a state of life overflowing with life force, wisdom, compassion, joy and eternity. We are all Buddhas, unawakened to this fact.

The purpose of the Buddha's advent was to awaken all people to the Thus Come One residing within their own hearts.

At the conclusion of this ceremony, all these innumerable beings promise to appear in the world after the Buddha's death and to spread this great Truth and Law far into the future.

In 1844, in the January issue of the Dial magazine, the publication of the New England Transcendentalist Club, Henry David Thoreau, one of the great bards of the American Renaissance, introduced a translation of the 'Parable of the Medicinal Herbs' chapter of the Lotus Sutra, the core and heart of all the Buddhist teachings, to the American public.

His article went mostly unnoticed, but the way had been opened for those legions of lovers of this world to appear, messengers forged upon the anvil of eternal life, donning the garb now of unknown, unheard-of people, the cabinet maker, the farmer, the steel worker, the secretary, bartender, caretaker, seamstress, machinist, railroad worker, pharmacist, lifeguard, a million identities, superb actors and actresses from time immemorial now appearing upon this grand stage of America, you would never imagine they carried forth the secret, the joy, the message, the hope, the future unimaginable, the power, expressing in their very lives invincible proof, singing tunes, swelling a grand chorus of jubilation.

Thoreau opened the door, and now they appear. They are here to construct a new myth of America.

Who are these people?

They are you and I.

GANGS OF THE KOSMOS

"There will soon be no more priests. Their work is done. They may wait awhile, perhaps a generation or two, dropping off by degrees. A superior breed shall take their place, the gangs of kosmos and prophets en masse shall take their place. A new order shall arise and they shall be the priests of man, and every man shall be his own priest. The churches built under their umbrage shall be the churches of men and women. Through the divinity of themselves shall the kosmos and the new breed of poets be interpreters of men and women and of all events and things. They shall find their inspiration in real objects today, symptoms of the past and future. They shall not deign to defend immortality or God or the perfection of things or liberty or the exquisite beauty and reality of the soul. They shall arise in America and be responded to from the remainder of the earth."

-- Walt Whitman.
Preface to Leaves of Grass.

THOMAS PAINE

"These are the times that try men's souls."

So wrote Thomas Paine in 1776 at the beginning of the American Revolutionary War.

His words from "The Crisis" were read to the demoralized and hungry troops of General George Washington just before Christmas, 1776, and his words stirred the soldiers morale.

The pamphlet continued:

"Tyranny, like hell, is not easily conquered; yet we have this consolation with us, that the harder the conflict, the more glorious the triumph. What we obtain too cheap, we esteem too lightly; it is dearness only that gives every thing its value. Heaven knows how to put a proper price upon its goods; and it would be strange indeed if so celestial an article as freedom should not be highly rated."

Two days later Washington's troops crossed the Delaware River and completely routed a thousand of the enemy.

Another of his pamphlets, "Common Sense", advocating independence from England, sold an estimated 500,000 copies, which, out of a population of about 2,000,000 free persons, made it the best selling book ever. John Adams reportedly said, "Without the pen of the author of 'Common Sense', the sword of Washington would have been raised in vain."

Not as well known, though, is that Tom Paine wrote another pamphlet - one that had an enormous impact upon readers of his time.

It was called "The Age of Reason."

Paine was a Deist, a philosophy valuing reason and observation of the natural world as the basis for religious beliefs.

He wrote:

"I believe in the equality of man; and I believe that religious duties consist in doing justice, loving mercy, and endeavoring to make our fellow creatures happy.

"But lest it should be supposed that I believe many other things in addition to these, I shall, in the progress of this work, declare the things I do not believe, and my reasons for not believing them.

"I do not believe in the creed professed by the Jewish Church, by the Roman Church, by the Greek Church, by the Turkish Church, by the Protestant Church, nor by any church that I know of. My own mind is my own church.

"All national institutions of churches, whether Jewish, Christian or Turkish, appear to me no other than human inventions, set up to terrify and enslave mankind, and monopolize power and profit."

These were strong words in his day, and they are still strong words.

Not tolerating tyranny in the political realm, Paine would suffer no such tyranny in the religious realm.

The intent behind his words was not to malign individuals; but rather to free humanity of age-old shackles of the mind and spirit.

The individual was his focus. Freedom was his focus. Bringing forth the unfettered and unlimited potential of the individual was his focus.

Now we are in the midst of another revolution. A new world is being born, a new America, and a new American experience.

Revolutions, both political and spiritual, are transforming our world. Old forms and tyrannies of the mind are dissolving into chaos and dust, paving the way for new and more grandiose shoots of being.

Amid this fracturing of our world, a new spiritual foundation is needed and required.

It is a religion beyond the old tribal mentalities, us and them. It is a religion broad enough to include every man, woman and child on the planet. It is a religion connected to the cosmos, yet based on reason.

This new religion is emerging everywhere on our planet. It is emerging among Christians, among Jews, among Muslims, among Hindus and Buddhists, atheists and agnostics. It is a religion beyond all these creeds. It is the prelude to, and necessary foundation of, a great new emerging civilization.

Thomas Paine's work was a harbinger of this new age and civilization. It was a bold thrust into the future.

He was a great patriot, a courageous American, and a great visionary.

He summed up his faith in one sentence:

"The world is my country, all mankind are my brethren, and to do good is my religion."

DREAM BIG

Power invests in the self.

As long as you navigate the circumference, who you are and who you dream to be remain unexpressed.

The center of the circle is at the center.

Unleashing this self requires courage and boldness. It requires faith. We are here to unleash the genius and power of our universe.

It requires not one cent.

You need no one to help you.

Everything is within your life, waiting to be summoned and expressed.

Who are you?

You are the impassioned dream within your heart.

No one can chart the course for you.

You are the only one who knows the way.

You are as big as the universe. The universe is your ally.

Recognize who you are.

Dream big. Let the dream come forth.

_____

SOJOURNER TRUTH

"That man over there says that women need to be helped into carriages, and lifted over ditches, and to have the best place everywhere. Nobody ever helps me into carriages, or over mud-puddles, or gives me any best place! And ain't I a woman? Look at me! Look at my arm! I have ploughed and planted, and gathered into barns, and no man could head me! And ain't I a woman? I could work as much and eat as much as a man - when I could get it - and bear the lash as well! And ain't I a woman? I have borne thirteen children, and seen most all sold off to slavery, and when I cried out with my mother's grief, none but Jesus heard me! And ain't I a woman?"

-- Sojourner Truth.
African-American abolitionist and women's rights activist; born into the horrors of slavery, she later traveled and spoke widely for an end to slavery and women's rights.

LIFE AND DEATH

Death.

We have been skirting the issue ever since the white man came to America and buried the Indians in the mud and rivers.

These aboriginals were unafraid of death, they built huge fires and smoked the pipe, but as the darkness closed in and the moon hung like a lantern pointing the way in the sky, they were unafraid, it was part of the living world around them, the animals, the sun rising each morning, thunder and lightning and darkness and rain, and then the clouds parting and sunshine brilliant as the beginning of time.

It was life and death, and the great circle come to a close.

And always the light appearing once again, like a small sliver and crack of dawn, life come back again, and the rain washing the sky clean, and horses and bison standing stark still in the soft shimmering morning light, the whole world silent and beautiful, and the wonder of it all, the freshness and dew.

But even the Indians lost their hearts. They built casinos, they traded the heart of the world for blackjack winnings and five-card stud, and copied it all and stuck everything in the face of the white man, and made piles of winnings and invested and bought out whole towns, but lost in the end - the flow of life of the great spirit running through their veins - lost it all on a throw of the dice.

A new story, a new myth now takes shape, something new, never seen before.

Life and death, moving about one another, twin universes of joy.

Simple things. Growing aware of the light around us. Trees and birds and ourself suspended in space. Three and four and five dimensions of an astonishing world, and we are here, we have been honored out of all time and space to occupy this moment, this living breathing moment which will never come again, friends' voices, a touch on the arm, to feel our heart beating, remembering all those who came before, the billions and trillions, this moment waited for and fought for and endured for by generations unending, this moment in America, this time of eternity.

It has always been here, but we were unaware.

We looked into each other's eyes, but there was no mirror. We sought ourselves in the forests and in the hills and over the oceans, along a maze of streets, in lovers, in frenzies of desire, but there was no one there.

Out of the gathering chaos emerges a new world, a world of people tied to each other by bonds of the heart, a new world beyond borders, beyond nations, beyond nationality and religion and race and ethnicity, a world and a people alive to who they are, brothers and sisters of the cosmos, appearing here and now in eternity.

———————————

WE OPEN THE WAY

Wandering through the small, lonely towns of early America.

There was Sherwood Anderson, and his small Ohio towns. There was Theodore Dreiser, and Sister Carrie, and a vision of life that portrayed eternity in the passing of seemingly insignificant lives. There was Thomas Wolfe, with his haunting images of America, his hunger for life and America, his wanting to possess it all, to capture it forever, the very heart of America. And F. Scott Fitzgerald, and his figure of Gatsby, who embodied the beauty and tragedy and sense of loss of the American Dream as no other figure in American literature ever has, before or since.

I love you all. You nourished me. You fed the dream of myself, and roused a dream of life here in America that evoked the sadness and beauty of the vast passing landscape, the fleeting moments, the passing of innumerable lives, yet all within the ordinariness of something eternal. You searched for the key, the lost words, the open sesame that would unlock the heart and meaning of it all, yet never found it. You carved words onto endless pages, trying to grasp something, that elusive something moving your characters inexorably towards death, the vast panorama of life and death, and never a way to unlock it all. We owe you such a debt for your beautiful words. They showed the way. They hinted at the secret.

With you in our heart now, we open the way.

DEMOCRACY

What is democracy?

Here in the United States, in what we consider the world's most perfect democracy, political parties are at each other's throats, struggling to gain fifty-one percent of the vote, or fifty-one percent of the power, so that one party and its adherents can control and have their way with the other forty-nine percent of the electorate who are out of power.

When Nelson Mandela was a young boy in South Africa, tribal decisions were made in a different manner.

The tribes came together periodically, and the Chief of the tribes was forced to listen for days to peoples' ideas and criticism - even of himself, without responding. When all opinions and ideas had been presented, the Chief would then make decisions based upon those opinions.

But this did not end the decision making process. For it was not until further discussion and voting had taken place and everyone felt satisfied - in other words, one hundred percent agreement - that the new plans were then put into action.

Mandela wrote:

"Democracy meant all men were to be heard, and a decision was taken together as a people. Majority rule was a foreign notion. A minority was not to be crushed by a majority."

Such humanity, in what we might think of as a backward culture, puts our own bickering and posturing for position and
power to shame.

———————————————

THE MOST LOVED PERSON

The Buddha once said:

"You can search throughout the entire universe for someone who is more deserving of your love and affection than you are yourself, and that person is not to be found anywhere. You yourself, as much as anybody in the entire universe, deserve your love and affection."

―――――――――――――

I AM AMERICA

I am America.

Once again, I open up vast prairies and rivers roaring down from mountains. The bison return, thundering upon the plains.

I am the voices of all those who have come before.

Indian Chief Seattle:

"To us the ashes of our ancestors are sacred and their resting place is hallowed ground. You white men wander far from the graves of your ancestors and seemingly without regret. Your religion was written upon tablets of stone by the iron finger of your God so that you could not forget. The Red Man could never comprehend or remember it. Our religion is the traditions of our ancestors - the dreams of our old men, given them in solemn hours of the night by the Great Spirit; and the visions of our sachems, and is written in the hearts of our people.

"Your dead cease to love you and the land of their nativity as soon as they pass the portals of the tombs and wander away beyond the stars. They are soon forgotten and never return. Our dead never forget this beautiful world that gave them being.

"They still love its verdant valleys, its murmuring rivers, its magnificent mountains, sequestered vales and verdant lined lakes and bays, and ever yearn in tender fond affection over the lonely hearted living, and often return from the happy hunting ground to visit, guide, console and comfort them."

I am America.

Ships with cargoes of black humanity, stolen from the arms of mother Africa, cramped in sickening holds for weeks upon the waves, many dying, brought to a new land, desecrated, treated abominably, ground under the heel and the whip, yet surviving, enduring beyond enduring, infusing new blood into this seething cauldron of a newly coalescing America.

I am America.

Soldiers with their faces dead in the dirt at Gettysburg, Shiloh, Fredericksburg, Antietam, Vicksburg, who had dreams of living, of loving, but whose dreams were buried one day beneath an uncaring sky, cannon smoking, blood running in rivers down fields, drenching the land, soaking deep into the earth, hearts of brothers broken upon the mythic anvil of America.

President Abraham Lincoln:

"Fondly do we hope, fervently do we pray, that this mighty scourge of war may speedily pass away. Yet, if God wills that it continue until all the wealth piled by the bondsman's two hundred and fifty years of unrequited toil shall be sunk, and until every drop of blood drawn with the lash shall be paid by another drawn with the sword, as was said three thousand years ago, so still it must be 'the judgments of the Lord are true and righteous altogether.'"

I am America.

Immigrants from around the earth, sick and desperate and crowded up like cattle on ships, and then they looked up and saw Lady Liberty and her torch of freedom and it was like something out of a dream, it took their breath away. They endured filthy tenements, they endured everything you could imagine, the remembrance of Liberty graven forever and beckoning in their hearts.

Sweat-soaked men in Pittsburg and Youngstown and East Chicago and Gary working in belching fire pits casting great coils of steel, dipping into acid baths, the air taking away everyone's breath, rolling out tons of metal, day after day, twelve hours a day, seven days a week, no respite, no recourse, trapped in a hell of monotony and white hot heat and sweat for dollars to feed wife and children.

They go unremembered, but I remember. I am America.

I am the Dream that all of them sought.

Millions piling up their bodies in war.

An agony of blighted dreams - for what? To foster a greater dream? What if the greater dream was a nightmare? What if it was a lie? What if the bodies rotting into the earth were mulch for more wars?

The human heart - what agony and joy! What betrayal and murder and love and laying down one's life for another, for an idea, for a way of life, for money, for God, for man and woman and child.

And all of this buried in the graves of untold billions and trillions and quadrillions - for the world goes back farther than anyone ever imagined - of silenced voices and blunted dreams and aspirations noble and ignoble, all dragged down into death, a vast black hole in the heart of the universe emitting no light deep into space beyond time, but coming out now a wormhole on the other side, intact, all the hell and misery and clawing and pain and unforgiven anger at the shortness of time, a cry of new birth, seeing the light once again, all the voices, all the dreams, carrying forth in syncopated rhythm a new music upon the plains and valleys of this mythical continent called America.

The trees, the voices, the bison, the incredible skies, the dead, the living, war and peace, love and hatred, typhoons and earthquakes and suns and stars in the heavens - I am them all.

I am America.

My name resounds across corridors of time and space.

I boldly announce my identity.

I am America. I am forever.

_____

PIONEERS

"The American Dream can no more remain static than can the American nation. We cannot any longer take an old approach to world problems. They aren't the same problems. It isn't the same world. We must not adopt the methods of our ancestors; instead, we must emulate that pioneer quality in our ancestors that made them attempt new methods for a New World."

-- Eleanor Roosevelt.

THE STAR IS YOU

America means to show the unlimited possibilities of a single human being. We are met here to enact this drama.

The star is you. The star is me.

I can be a street sweeper and confound worlds.

This is the true meaning of democracy.

_____

OPPORTUNITY

How do you forge a way ahead when all corridors are closed, when nothing moves, when all the locks have no keys?

This is the point of opportunity.

Opportunity resides in your heart and mind, nowhere else.

Bend to the task, it will open. New synapses will fire in your brain, new energies course through your blood.

Never give up on the dream. Never give up on the dream.

And move. And move.

And never give up on the dream.

_____

THE HEAVENS ARE ANGRY

Without a doubt, the heavens are angry.

Drought, fires, torrential rain, record snow and cold, hurricanes, tornadoes, demonic winds - a certain wildness and derangement seems let loose upon the mountains and plains and towns and coasts of America.

Identities are being fragmented.

Is it God who is angry? Are we at that turning in point in history, an Armageddon?

Whole families and communities hoard up food and water, build walls and encasements against the coming chaos.

But still, there are no answers. There is no splitting of the skies or parting of the waters, no final curtain calls announcing the end of days. Only a deafening silence, a hollow absence of being, punctuated by the electric sound of crickets massing before the storm.

It was the same a thousand, five thousand, thirty thousand years ago. Wait, and wait, but never an answer.

We have come to the answer now, here in America.

It is a flower about to blossom in the desert.

All around is the gathering chaos, yet tiny buds of lovely being are poking through the ground, in this place, in that place, they are as yet unknown faces, young mothers, young boys and girls, working fathers, you would never imagine they carried forth an answer to the riddles of all time, to the Sphinx puzzles, to the Delphi oracles, to the Holy Grail quests, that they carried within their simple, ordinary, day-to-day orbit the key to Job's lament, and the philosopher's stone and magic words to open up the caves of Sesame.

It is all beginning here.

Some would praise the Lord, but let us here praise instead the charwoman, the chimney sweep, the subway mechanic, the dog trainer, the house painter, as well as a thousand, and ten thousand, and millions of other ordinary, extraordinary and unknown people who lavish their heart and soul upon others with no thought of return, who spend their days and nights, year after year, giving of themselves for the future and a better world.

They are here, among us. They have always been here.

Anger will turn to rapture. The tumultuous wrath of the heavens will subside, and turn to a soft, quiet wind.

It all comes from within the heart. All the hell and all the heaven, all the storms and disruption and insanity and wild winds and tortuous crashing waves and torrential rain and nightmares of ocean and unrelenting blazing blistering sun, all come from the human heart, everything mirroring our compassion.

Thus it has always been.

One person the key, one person, struggling in the darkness and depths with demons and monsters and giant fire-breathing dragons.

Don Quixote tilting with windmills, with illusions, with phantoms of the mind that bind us to a wheel of suffering - all of them assuming their posts, as autocrats and politicians sucking away the peoples' power, as thoughts and ideas that bind our hands and cast us bleeding and helpless upon the ground, as words and blows that devalue everything we have ever been, demolishing hope, destroying self-worth, ignoring the god within in exchange for obeisance to false gods without.

Temples and monuments, tyrannical codes of law, iron rule, priestly classes, false philosophies, heartless subjugation, division, slaughtering of the heart, armed camps, atomic and hydrogen bombs, annihilation, ethnic cleansing, corruption, tribe mentalities, brutality, desecration of the environment, desecration of our worth, desecration of our life - windmills all of monsters that need slaying, laid to by the sword, rooted out with spades and root poison, and salt spread into the very ground from which they grew and subverted our minds and hearts.

This is the task.

One person transforms himself or herself, and monstrous black holes, weighing billions of suns, grow quiet.

A new breed emerging, honoring our image in the mirror, recognizing the source of power, never again giving it away to anyone or anything, cultivating respect of oneself and others, knowing we are all connected, loving life, loving the struggle, becoming all that one can be to encourage others to become all that they can be, laughing and dancing now, proud of the source, recognizing divinity in oneself and in all, propelled into a grand trajectory of immense good fortune.

Let the flowers bloom. Let grasses rejoice.

Let the winds and seas and sun and rain and darkness and light conspire to praise the men and women on this round of earth.

This is America as it is becoming.

OUR COMMON HUMANITY

"For we know that our patchwork heritage is a strength, not a weakness. We are a nation of Christians and Muslims, Jews and Hindus, and non-believers. We are shaped by every language and culture, drawn from every end of this Earth; and because we have tasted the bitter swill of civil war and segregation, and emerged from that dark chapter stronger and more united, we cannot help but believe that the old hatreds shall someday pass; that the lines of tribe shall soon dissolve; that as the world grows smaller, our common humanity shall reveal itself; and that America must play its role in ushering in a new era of peace."

-- Barack Obama.

WOMEN

Any religion, philosophy, or mode of thinking that denigrates women, that treats women unequally, has no place in the future of America, or of the world.

_____

NEWGRANGE

It is Christmas time again all across America.

Memories crowd upon the stage, fondness brushes the heart strings, carols sung upon the immense darkened prairie, harkening back to times past.

The Christian world celebrates this day as the birthday of Jesus Christ, but the facts do not corroborate this.

Roman pagans first introduced the holiday of Saturnalia, a week of general drunkenness and lawlessness, that was celebrated between December 17th and the 25th; and in the fourth century, A.D., Christianity absorbed the holiday in an effort to bring along the masses who still celebrated the Saturnalia. Even Christmas trees, mistletoe, and Santa Claus had their origins in pagan times and cultures.

The date generally marks the winter solstice also; and I can more easily find meaning in this correspondence with the movements of the sun and heavens.

Several years ago, I visited the Newgrange mound in Ireland, an extraordinary prehistoric monument, consisting of alternating layers of earth and stones, with grass on top. The mound was built around 3200 B.C., predating even Stonehenge and the great pyramids of Giza in Egypt.

The mound is 250 feet across and 40 feet high.

A passageway on the southeast side of the monument leads into the mound, and about a third of the way in are three small chambers off a larger central chamber, with a high vault roof.

On the winter solstice, generally December 21st of each year, the rising sun inches slowly down the passageway for about seventeen minutes in an advancing beam of light that eventually reaches and illuminates the central chamber of the mound. The ceremony is re-enacted for tourists with the aid of electric lights.

There are many conflicting theories about the meaning of all of this. Obviously, though, the people at that time had an extraordinary knowledge of the movement of the heavenly bodies, and the solstice ceremony undoubtedly had religious meanings and overtones.

One of the guides on my trip there hinted at an interpretation, though, that rang true to me.

The winter solstice signaled a rebirth, the longest night of the year turning once again towards spring.

At this moment, the sun's beam moved along the darkened passageway, penetrating the mound of the earth, and climaxing in a burst of light and conception at the heart of the Earth itself.

Sun and Earth were joined in the act of creation. The seed of a rebirth of life and fertility had been planted, promising the fruition of the people and the land.

The three small chambers off the main one were thought to have held the burial remains of deceased human beings. These remains participated in the rebirth of the Earth and of light and were also reborn. Newgrange was a miniature of a vision of rebirth and eternal life.

These ancient, unknown peoples were more in tune with the rhythms of nature than we are. They sensed deeply the universal connections, and they saw behind the daily movements of sun and moon and stars the operation of something ineffable, a reflection of their own lives.

This same connection we need to re-acquire - this time, though, with man and woman at the center.

Not looking beyond ourselves for the wonder, the power, but revealing them from within our own minds and hearts.

_____

MOVER OF SUNBEAMS

Who am I?

Mover of sunbeams, dispenser of fire and light and dark, creator waiting to happen. Once awakened, my every glance, every thought, manifesting in ripples of creation reverberating throughout time and space, permeating birds and animals and men and women and the rings of Saturn, the brooding rock of Pluto, and moving beyond into everything past, present and future, multiple universes, multiple times, everything that ever was or will be.

This is my life. This is your life.

Praise be to our lives.

_____

THE REALM OF ETERNITY

There is a realm of life that no one knows about, or fathoms, or sees.

This is the realm of Eternity, which exists right here, right now, in the most mundane affairs that go on day to day.

Even modern physics hints at this.

It is two parallel universes, each mirroring the other, though one is a movement through shadows and shades, and the other, an arena of joy.

We live in a world of shadows. It is Plato all over again, and shadows on the wall in the cave.

Plato was dealing with words and concepts, though, and this world of light and reality is here and now, but unbeknownst to everyone.

Once awakened to this parallel world, suffering turns to joy, complaint turns to jubilant expectation, life itself becomes a wonderment and a jewel.

We ourselves are the wonderment. Our bodies, our minds, our hands and eyes are themselves this hidden universe.

Stars and nebulae and countless suns coursing through our

blood, countless beings arrayed in our hair, our heart at the center, radiating emanations, vast reflections in the mirror.

The clerk in the store has blond hair, blue eyes. She is polite. She puts figures into the computer. Another sale. A line of three people stand waiting.

This woman has two sons, age five and three. Her mother helps with the baby sitting. Her mother, age fifty-nine, is from Russia. Her parents and grandparents go back to the time of the Revolution. Her grandfather disappeared into Siberia and was never heard from again. Vast hordes of horsemen swarmed over the steppes, slaughtering everyone in sight, burning everything to the ground. Lone herdsmen tracked for aeons the reindeer, moving glacially the line of human development a mile, two miles to the east, then dropping down through glacial passageways, down through the plains and mountains, building fires all along the prairie. And beyond, in caves and mounds of stone and earth oriented toward the rising winter solstice sun, the sun's rays penetrated the mound of the earth and lit up with a shaft of light the interior chamber, fructifying the earth, lending sparks of life to the broken, decaying bones of men and women and children re-invented by the light.

All of this five thousand years ago.

And the woman stands there, at the checkout stand, punching numbers in the computer, and her body holds the unexpressed voices of thousands, of the dead and gone and unremembered, and never a hint, never the fire of a thought that in her living body there roam the herdsmen and reindeer and sacrificial ceremonies of waves of mothers and fathers and sisters and brothers.

This is the world unremembered, unknown, unimagined. It lives and breathes in her very own body, yet only as a shadow memory, and she has the power to bring it all to life again, she has the power to move in another realm where everything comes to life again, reindeer, mammoths, murderers, suns, moons, but she keeps punching numbers into the computer, and people file by, and they look at each other momentarily not recognizing the companion who painted images of bison and elk and bears together upon caverns deep in the earth twenty thousand years ago, it is all a shadow world, a parallel universe of the heart, unawakened.

All of this lies asleep. We pass each other in the dream world. Two universes side by side.

And where do we really live?

_____

THE GOAL OF LIFE

"The experience of eternity right here and now is the function of life. Heaven is not the place to have the experience; here is the place to have the experience.

"The goal of life is to make your heartbeat match the beat of the universe, to match your nature with Nature."

-- Joseph Campbell.

_____

UPON THE BATTLEMENTS

There is a power in us that something does not want us to know.

At every turn, illusion masks the way. Dark stirrings in our mind, doubts, and signs everywhere warning of danger and loss and impossibility.

In olden times, it was dragons, breathing fire and hate, that barred the way. Or monstrous serpents and quicksand dragging us down to hellish bottoms. Or snarling dogs and huge spiders and pits of burning oil.

Today it is more mundane dragons - loss of home, fear of finances, a shattering of relationships - but at the core, it is the same illusion, the same betrayal of the dream that bleeds our heart and courage, the same diminishing of our own faith in our own power.

So it has always been. The myths of old tell the same old story.

We are myth makers in our own right, this very day, this very hour, poised upon the battlements, sword in hand, slaying illusions one after the other, never giving in. Though desperate and facing overwhelming odds and weary in arm, still holding forever the dream aloft in reverence.

There comes a point when everything will turn.

Hold on.

LIBERTY

"How many dawns, chill from his rippling rest
The seagull's wings shall dip and pivot him,
Shedding white rings of tumult, building high
Over the chained bay waters Liberty--"

-- Hart Crane
To Brooklyn Bridge

RELIGION

What is religion?

This is a question that has to be resolved, and it is a question of the utmost importance for America, and for the world.

A great worldwide democracy and new world order simply cannot come into being without a corresponding great spiritual revolution as its foundation.

Vaclav Havel, former president of the Czech Republic, who knew something of revolutions, stated his opinion that, currently, democratic societies were afflicted with materialism and a frenzied consumerism.

He asked:

"Wherein lies that forgotten dimension of democracy that could give it universal resonance?"

And he answers:

"If democracy is not only to survive but to expand successfully and resolve those conflicts of cultures, then, in my opinion, it must rediscover and renew its own transcendental origins. It must renew its respect for that non-material order which is not only above us but also in us and among us, and which is the only possible and reliable source of man's respect for himself, for others... The authority of a world democratic order simply cannot be built on anything else but the revitalized authority of the universe."

What is this "authority of the universe?"

It is the all-embracing heart and mind of Life itself.

What we are heading for is the dawning of a great new spiritual civilization - a civilization unprecedented in the long annals of history. This will be the time of the true awakening to the unbounded potential within each individual and within the race as a whole. All the prior factions and divisions - ethnicities, nationalities - must give way before recognition of the greatness of the common, unadorned human being. This recognition can only be revealed through the unfolding of a great new spiritual phase of the human race.

Albert Einstein, a man of reason and science, yet a person who stood in awe of the mystery of the universe around us, wrote:

"A human being is part of the whole - called by us 'Universe' - a part limited in time and space. He experiences himself, his thoughts and feelings as something separated from the rest - a kind of optical delusion of his consciousness. This delusion is a kind of prison for us, restricting us to our personal desires and affection for a few persons nearest us. Our task must be to free ourselves from this prison by widening our circle of compassion to embrace all living creatures and the whole of nature in its beauty. Nobody is able to achieve this completely but striving for such achievement is, in itself, a part of the liberation and a foundation for inner security."

What is needed is democracy, yes. But the democratic revolution the world is headed for and pining for can never come to fruition without a corresponding spiritual revolution that breaks down the old walls of our limited perception and reconnects all of our lives to the life of all of humanity and to the cosmos itself.

This is a democracy beyond all distinctions.

This is democracy that demolishes poverty and sickness and unhappiness by prioritizing the welfare of the individual human being as the focus of all our endeavors, in economics, politics, and education. This is a democracy that empowers people, and destroys war itself, for every other person in the world is no longer seen as "the other", but rather as an integral part of our own life.

Much of the world's agony in our times can be traced directly to religion.

Look only at the Middle East: The birthplace of three great religious traditions, Judaism, Christianity, and Islam.

People there are locked in anger, hatred, dispute, war, killing, because of religion. At the root is religion, and the separation caused by religious beliefs, which makes one man and woman different from another man and woman; which divides them; which breeds a separate tribal identity that causes one man to look at another as "the other", even though they all have the same human face and visage and feelings and emotions and dreams.

This same scenario of religion against religion is playing out all over the globe.

Religion is dividing people. Religion is crippling people. Religion is destroying people.

This is not religion in any true sense of the word; and this is not a religion that can be the basis for a true democracy in this land of America.

A young boy, after reading about the battles of religion in his local newspaper, was quoted recently as saying:

"We need a new religion."

This new religion is already upon us.

It is manifesting even now in the lives of Christians, Jews, Muslims, Hindus, Buddhists, atheists, agnostics - in all of those who are waking to the Truth about humanity and our place in the cosmos and to the interconnectedness of all life.

It is the individual coming to the fore. It is the power and potential of one person.

No one can claim authority over this potential. It can only be drawn forth by the individual himself or herself. Each person is a master and creator of his or her own destiny. All power is in one's own hands.

To denigrate that potential, to subvert that power, to demand submission, to create persons and institutions of worship placed far above the people, is a travesty and utter warping of the true function of religion.

We need to re-connect individual human beings once again, in all their diversity, to the Law of Life that is at the core of everyone's existence, the basic groundwork of being that permeates everything, within and without, and that reveals our original roots in a common humanity.

In other words, what is needed is a new spiritual dimension, a dimension that transcends our smaller identities, and opens our lives to a truer identity at one with the life of the universe itself.

Too long this has gone on, and now, after the passing of innumerable generations, the world, and America especially, is poised for a rebirth - precursor to a civilization that requires an entirely new spiritual orientation for the generations to come.

At the center of this spirituality is the recognition of the worth and value of each human being on the face of the Earth. At the heart of this spirituality is a recognition-in-fact of the essential oneness of humanity.

We do not know who we are.

We ourselves are the gods whom we have worshipped upon the altars stretching back to immemorial times. We are the very ones.

72

Never knowing the source of our own heart, we have bowed down to countless graven powers, never recognizing our image in the mirror.

The "authority of the universe" is that call to overcome our own circumscribed ego, to break down the walls of the heart, to recognize ourselves in others, to recognize our own greatness, to fashion new and radical myths of time and space in which we take our place finally upon the stage of forever.

The universe we live in is immortal. And there are universes of universes beyond our own.

We are immortal in this land.

REACH FOR THE STARS

"Every great dream begins with a dreamer. Always remember, you have within you the strength, the patience, and the passion to reach for the stars to change the world."

-- Harriet Tubman.
African-American abolitionist, humanitarian, and campaigner for women's suffrage.

_____

OMNIPRESENT URGE

The universe is built in such a way that one person mirrors the universe, inconceivable in its potential and power, and all people together mirror countless inconceivable universes, powers infinitely surpassing galactic sun-storms and the nuclear fusion of stars.

But we languish here, on this blue planet, mired down in suffering.

Seven billion of us struggling and starving and clawing and hating and fighting for everything to be solely our own. Resisting the omnipresent urge within us to become as large as the universe itself.

_____

THE ORIGINALS

Yes, now this retinue from the Lotus Sutra, this gang of enlightened beings down from the mountaintop of eternity, appear among us.

They are everywhere you look, spreading a new vision of life, the power and greatness of the people.

We had thought them something special, this galactic band of revolutionaries.

But they had no real distinct identities. They were embodiments of a state of life - purity, steadfastness, eternity, joy, wisdom, compassion - attributes of a great new emerging life and civilization.

Reveal their names now: John, Jim, Harry, Joan, Jack, Marie, Louise. You see them walking down any street in America.

It is a new world being born.

All these multitudes gathered within the Treasure Tower, they were present all along within our own lives.

They were you and I.

I remember the lightning, the flashes of illumination, like the brightness of day in the darkness, and the faces of brothers and sisters as far as the eye could see. We were there forever. The galaxies and universes were our home, vast to explore, vast to roam in, vast to play out countless dramas and scenarios, forever and forever, no end. And now finally come home, finally upon this Earth, this core and center of the infinite cosmos.

What joy! What immense good fortune!

We are the originals. We were there from the beginning. We attended the ceremony, we heard the words.

The words became ourselves, became trees and grasses, fed the animals, and the animals fell to our knives and entered our blood and became our thoughts and words and created the world and a billion and trillion of others followed and opened up a million mirrors of worlds and universes, each with someone like you and I at the center, and we never guessed that we were the originators, all of time hung on our whims, all of space expanded to our touch, so let our hearts true intent and purpose man the wheel and guide us into new and glorious seas.

Awaiting others now, awaiting young men and women, bold the vision in their eyes, leading the way to America.

———————————

THE KEY

Here in America, we have not yet found the connection. We have no key to the world around us.

When I was a young man, I worked for several months as a bartender at a lake resort.

One man came in almost every night. He drank heavily, staying for hours, yet still retained a sharp, steely clarity about him.

He would talk about many things, but invariably he would end by talking about fishing.

He described the fishing he had done that week, or last weekend, or last year, or even decades ago.

He described different baits, tackle, his knowledge of the topography of the land below the waters, the final catch, the weight and length of the fish, the look of the fish, the scales and eyes, the different fins, the sheen on the body of the fish.

He went on and on.

As he spoke, his voice grew more animated, his hands moved with excitement, as though trying to shape and describe something he sensed and felt but was unable to express.

It was all about fishing and fish.

It seemed to me he was trying to get to the heart of something, pushing ever deeper, in repetition, almost expecting some kind of revelation to break forth from the body of the fish itself.

Years later, I visited Aix-en-Provence in southern France, where the great painter Paul Cezanne lived and worked. I drove out to a promontory overlooking Mt. Sainte Victoire, the mountain that Cezanne loved to paint.

I heard that Cezanne sometimes painted in a kind of frenzy and fury.

He painted the mountain over and over, trying to capture something from the mute mass of rock, structuring his paints and drawings to capture the essence of the picture before him, but with anger, because the mountain or the sky or the land or whatever it was would not yield up to him its secret.

It must have been a travail of the heart.

I thought about the man in the bar, and his stories of fish, and I think he was looking for the same revelation. He wanted light to break forth like suns from the scales and body of the fish.

The light was there, but Cezanne and the drunken man did not have the key.

———————————

A MUSHROOM CLOUD OF MADNESS

Hiroshima, bombs, atomic bombs, hydrogen bombs, neutron bombs, annihilation of the other, black and white, us and them, the betrayers and the betrayed, good and bad, God and the Devil, the chosen ones and the damned, heaven and hell, sin and redemption, life and death, miracles, saints and sinners, heterosexuals and homosexuals, Hindu and Muslim, Jew and Muslim, Christian and Muslim, mine and yours, this and that...

Seeds of destruction. Seeds of madness.

A mushroom cloud of madness.

—————————————

AMERICA'S EVERLASTING DREAM

"I believe we are lost here in America, but I believe we shall be found. And this belief, which mounts now to the catharsis of knowledge and conviction, is for me - and I think for all of us - not our only hope, but America's everlasting, living dream. I think the life which we have fashioned in America, and which has fashioned us - the forms we have made, the cells that grew, the honeycomb that was created - was self-destructive in its nature, and must be destroyed. I think these forms are dying, and must die, just as I know that America, and the people in it, are deathless, undiscovered, and immortal, and must live."

-- Thomas Wolfe
You Can't Go Home Again.

A SINGLE SOLITARY SOUL

Everything changes. Nothing stays. This is a truth of life.

Love is born and dies. Love turns to hatred and back again to love. Dark becomes light. Young becomes old. Stars and galaxies are born from the maws of gigantic black holes, live their day in seeming infinity, then explode as novas and are buried in the black nothingness of a dark, fecund universe.

What is the dream of one person against the limitless expanse of a seemingly uncaring universe?

Equal in immensity to the universe is the heart of one person. The universe can be made to bend to the wishes of a single solitary soul.

They are one in reality.

Gathering the very deepest intent of the universe itself into one's own heart, one can move the levers and power of infinite suns and stars and nebulae, and send tremors throughout the borders of time and space.

We all have this power.

It is only activated through a depth of compassion for all living beings commensurate with the physical extension of the universe itself.

_____

SONGS FROM SOMEWHERE

It's nice once in a while to sit back and listen to a little music.

The tunes percolate up from memory, they come wafting up from dark, hidden crevices of the night, permeating our bones and marrow, dampening the stress of the discordant day, a song like Paul McCartney's "Yesterday", which he said he had no idea from where it came or whose it was until no one else claimed the tune; like nuances, like soft pleadings from the shadows, from yesterday, from somewhere else and someone else softly whistling magic tunes from another time, another dimension, from the heart strings of the universe that is ever creating and making new tunes and exploring its own dimensions and time and meaning and trying to express a song of hope above the pain and struggle, a song however ephemeral to evoke the mystery, the ceaseless change, the poetry of something that can never be fixed and grasped but nevertheless is so poignant, we know it when we hear it, we understand, we cry, we weep, our heart strings vibrate to forgotten music, unremembered words, what is it we are looking for, why should our heart feel so deeply this beauty?

There must be another place where these songs live and breathe and grow and have substance, a time and place that pivots on eternity.

Or is it only in our own hearts and minds?

LIVE YOUR DREAMS

"Go confidently in the direction of your dreams. Live the life you've imagined."

"I have learned, that if one advances confidently in the direction of his dreams, and endeavors to live the life he has imagined, he will meet with a success unexpected in common hours."

-- Henry David Thoreau

———————————

CHANGING DESTINY

I remember walking along a sidestreet as a boy, in the small town I grew up in, and the snow crunched in ridges under my boots.

I remember riding my bicycle and turning up one of the streets, and the blaze of color from the leaves on the autumn trees was overwhelming. It was the most beautiful thing I had ever seen.

I remember the heat of summer, and the windbrakes separating the fields where we dug houses in the dirt and covered them with branches and leaves.

This was where I entered the world, this was where I began playing out the long script of life written in the stars and sun and moon, where the sap began moving, the leaves poking through the ground, budding out into a destiny prescribed by hidden pathways of life. The leaves became more leaves, the plant carried with it the seed of all plants, it became itself, it was all known from the beginning.

Was I known from the beginning? Did I become who I was all along?

We come into the world, and it is all shadows and illusions, playing in the fields, marching in the school band, reading books, wondering who we will become, trials and errors, slips and falls, gathering bits and pieces, a comet gathering little shards to itself as it flashes and hurtles through the void, destination unknown, yet on a trajectory, infallible, like the plant poking through the ground and becoming green leaves and beautiful flowers without a mind of its own, incapable of becoming anything but itself, its true self.

Am I the same? And who scripted and plotted out this universe of pathways?

I am the author. I am the play. I am the star.

I am America.

I go beyond the rude, mindless probing of life of the plant, of the rivers eating at the rocks for millennia, of the blind repetitions of dramas of life and love and victory and defeat, of endless stories that we have heard over and over again from beyond the stage of time itself.

I write stories never heard before upon the plains and mountains of America, I am the new singer, I sing new songs that awaken a new sun across the prairies and tall stacked cities, awakening at last, rubbing my eyes in the light.

I am America, becoming. I am the new song.

I am the song of every man and woman, awakened finally from the rude, dumb, insensate yearnings of life and death, of light and darkness, of black and white, round and square, ever and never, up and down, around and through, the very person standing in a new light, summoning joy and spreading it through the heart, penetrating vast worlds, rocketing past suns and orbs and galaxies arrayed like giant glowing horses against the dark of impenetrable night.

Now spin new tales.

Begin with the boy walking along a side street, snow crunching in ridges under his boots.

Add him riding his bicycle and being stunned by the beauty of autumn leaves.

Move him languorously through the summer heat and playhouses in the fields.

Then awaken in him Eternity.   Awaken in him all people. Awaken in him what has never been known.

Let him stride forth through the corridors of space and time, be forever here, let his heart issue forth from where everyone and everything issues forth, feel it pounding in his heart, gathering all fears and tears and sorrows and love and making it his own, his own heart gathering joy, never ceasing, always increasing, until mind and heart become one with everyone's universe.

Let this story come forth.   Let it be a story beyond time and becoming. Let it be forever.

Here in America.

———————————

HARD WORK

"We all have dreams. But in order to make dreams come into reality, it takes an awful lot of determination, dedication, self-discipline, and effort."

-- Jesse Owens.

Winner of four gold medals in track at the 1936 Olympics in Berlin, Germany. The most successful athlete at the Olympics, he spoiled Adolph Hitler's ideas of showcasing his Aryan ideals and prowess.

.

THE MIRACLE IS YOU

At the heart of the most pressing problem lies the key to turning everything around.

When the problem will not go away, when it stares you unrelentingly in the face, when you think you cannot go on living even unless it changes, this is the turning point.

But the problem will never change if you think something is going to magically happen, if you think the solution will arrive knocking at your door to give you relief, if you are waiting for the miracle to happen.

The miracle is you.

The miracle is summoning up totally new energies from within. It is forging new determinations, and then acting and moving ahead with all your might. It is do or die.

The miracle is finally believing in yourself. It is depending on no one and no thing. It is making up your mind.

It is calling forth infinite resources where you saw no resources.

The universe is waiting for you. The universe has given you this problem as a gift. The universe will bend to your every whim, but only when you yourself move with implacable will and determination.

It all depends on you.

You are the turning point of a miracle.

_____

THE REALM OF THE HEART

At present, the new civilization exists only in the hearts of men and women. But from the hearts of men and women will eventually arise new, unsurpassed structures of life.

The realm of the heart will take the place of everything. Not economics, not politics leading the way, but the heart. This is the path of development for the next several thousands of years, and forever.

SOMETHING NEW IS COMING

During the Great Depression of the 1930's in America, many people lost everything they had - jobs, homes, sense of security, even hope for the future.

Yet people survived. And a sense of community flourished in many cases. People were brought together by their common problems, they were forced to get back to basics and to things that really mattered. Pretenses were shed and destroyed. Bubbles burst and business empires collapsed.

Out of this bottoming out, though, emerged eventually the most dynamic and powerful country the world had ever seen.

We often forget our lessons learned, the past goes unremembered, and human desire takes precedence once again.

Now our foundations are being shaken once again - economic, political, social - a slide has commenced, and fear is in the wings.

Where are we going? Who are we? What does the future hold?

We are indeed entering a momentous time. It is tectonic plates shifting deep beneath our dreaming anxious world.

There is no going back. The old world is dying. And something new is coming.

Out of the gathering chaos will emerge a new world, a world of people tied to each other by bonds of the heart, beyond borders, beyond nations, beyond nationality and religion and race and ethnicity, a world and a people alive to who they are, brothers and sisters of the cosmos, appearing here and now in eternity.

It is coming. Make no mistake.

The heart of the universe is coming to fruition.

Here in America.

HERE I AM

To forget it all.
To love the sun.
To see the light brilliant on the hills.
To listen. To not move.
To bring Time to a stop amid the moment.
To breathe.
To feel Eternity.
To wonder. To remember.
To know. To feel.
Here I am.
Here I am.

_____

DEATH IS THE DREAMER

Death is the dreamer here in America.

Death is all around, along the boulevards, upwards to sky-scrapers, amidst the most mundane, apparently innocent actions, couples strolling in the park, hot dog stands, newspaper hawkers, boutique shops, the way the sun rises circumspectly over one part of town, barely noticed, bringing light to another day, shedding a harsh perspective to something buried and hidden deep in our lives, like shadows that follow our every step in the merciless, brilliant sunshine.

Are we dreaming here?

Rhythm of daytime reality and nighttime dreams. Short intervals of sunlight, and then drawn back irresistibly once again into a dream world, a chaos of fragmented, shifting memories, desires and impulses, in which we live again, though darkly, disconnected from linear time and motion.

Are we here or there? Why do we dream?

Is life itself a dream? Is death a waking from the dream of this life into the light of further dimensions?

Leo Tolstoy, the great Russian writer, in response to a letter from a friend, who had asked Tolstoy about his views on Buddhism and karma, replied:

"Just as we experience thousands of dreams in this life of ours, so is this life one of thousands of such lives which we enter into from the more real, actual, true life from which we come when we enter this life, and to which we return when we die.

"Our life is one of the dreams of that truer life. But even that truer life is only one of the dreams of another, even truer life and so on to infinity, to the one last true life, the life of God.

"Birth and the appearance of one's first notions of the world is a falling asleep and a most sweet sleep; death is an awakening.

"In the life which we call reality there is a semblance of love of one's neighbor. But in the life we came from and to which we are going the relationship is much closer, and love is no longer something to be desired, but something real. And in the ultimate life for which even that life is a dream, relationship and love are greater still.

"I would like you to understand me. I am not making it up to amuse myself. I believe in it, see it and know it for certain, and when I die I shall rejoice that I am waking up to that more real world of love."

And so we awaken from one world into another, here in America.

As the days and months and years go by, to realize that one holds the universe - suns and stars and moons and galaxies - within one's own heart. To feel shades and illusions peeling away, and the real world emerging before one's eyes, the deepening of the heart, the bonds of the heart spreading exponentially, reaching all of space and time, just a single human being embracing the world, seeing clearly now, reaching out forever.

Life and death, and moving about the axis of everything, revolving, changing, but fixed at the heart of the world.

A young woman pushes a carriage on the way to the market. Students carrying books, wait for the bus. Shops open, bins of produce inviting buyers. A businessman carrying a valise, walks hurriedly down the sidewalk.

People and places and facts that will never occur again. Death at the heart of everything, eating at the heart of the moment, life burgeoning forth at every moment, our own lives dying at each moment, birthing in the next moment, the play of light and dark, forever and never, being here and not being here, in and out, dreams and daylight, our lives refracting life and death, death giving meaning to the moment, death without which life cannot be, life and death dancing together in a cosmic dance around the taxi driver and the buses and people rushing past and lights changing green to yellow to red and back to green, and children and mothers and teachers and gardeners in the park, and the present changing to the past becoming the future, and through it all, even amid the pain and suffering and tears and frustrations and disappointments, a sense of wonderment, a deep-seated joy, an inexpressible prayer and bowing down and folding of one's hands in utter appreciation.

Life unfolding, and Death unfolding, and Eternity unfolding, finally, here in America.

WHAT WE COULD BE

"Always do what you are afraid to do."

"Hitch your wagon to a star."

"Once you make a decision, the universe conspires to make it happen."

"Our chief want is someone who will inspire us to be what we know we could be."

-- Ralph Waldo Emerson.

BELIEVE IN YOURSELF

There comes a time when you just have to hold on.

A small boat, amid giant waves, with no land in sight, the sun by day, but dense clouds and utter darkness at night. Now or never, it is victory or defeat, life or death.

Land must appear, or we are lost.

Time to summon forth a rallying cry. Believe in yourself! Hold fast to the boat of your dreams!

Life was made for dreams, and for the fulfilling of dreams. Within oneself is the universe, and all the powers of the universe, and all the powers needed to fulfill our dreams.

But we must hold fast, no matter what comes, high waves, typhoons, lightning, storms and torrential rain, waters boiling up from devilish depths.

There is only the tiny boat to hang onto, the self. There is nothing else.

Believe in yourself. Believe in your dreams.

A CROSS OF IRON

"Every gun that is made, every warship launched, every rocket fired signifies in the final sense, a theft from those who hunger and are not fed, those who are cold and are not clothed. This world in arms is not spending money alone. It is spending the sweat of its laborers, the genius of its scientists, the hopes of its children. This is not a way of life at all in any true sense. Under the clouds of war, it is humanity hanging on a cross of iron."

-- Dwight Eisenhower.

LIFE IS THE TREASURE

When everything in the universe is showing us miracles, is showing the way, is waiting breathlessly, is bursting with spring leaves and stars, is reverberating with song, is imagining pent-up blessings for us all; we drag through the day, we see nothing, hear nothing, feel nothing, we do not know that out of all the billions and trillions of lives that have preceded us, out of all the billions now on the planet, it is myself, it is you and I that have been singled out as special, the very ones, the most honored and praised and deserving of all.

Life is the treasure.

Nothing else can compare.

A WILLINGNESS OF THE HEART

"France was a land, England was a people, but America, having about it still that quality of the idea, was harder to utter - it was the graves at Shiloh and the tired, drawn, nervous faces of its great men, and the country boys dying in the Argonne for a phrase that was empty before their bodies withered. It was a willingness of the heart."

-- F. Scott Fitzgerald.

_____

AWAY WITH FUNDAMENTALISM

Away with fundamentalism.

Away with I am right and you are wrong.

All the strident dividing of humanity into this or that, the partitioning of men and women into us and them, the adherence to tribal gods, the enthroning of power and authority over people - away with all of this.

No quarter given. No intermediaries.

Bring forth the simple unadorned human being. Let us praise people.

The mother who diligently and painstakingly raises children; the father who holds down two jobs, sleeping four or five hours a night to support a family; those caring for the sick; students laboring through the night; janitors, health care workers, bus drivers, truckers, secretaries, farm workers, grocery clerks - all those in the background, all those unnoticed and underrated - bring them all to the fore now, this is their time, the spotlights swing around abruptly and illuminate infinite numbers of forgotten, unsung travelers throughout time.

They have been waiting for this curtain call.

Disappearing in their own place and time, they seemed to fade into darkness and oblivion; but you can walk through graveyards all over the globe, you can talk to the silent grave stones and think that no one hears, but they all hear, they hear every word of the living, they have been waiting for the time to reappear, not as ghosts, but as living flesh, reborn from the body of the universe that sends forth forever intimations of itself.

They were here with us all along.

At this centripetal point, they have no need for distorted and twisted cosmogonies.   They love life from the beginning, spawning songs of the universe, remembering the old beautiful light of sunlight on roofs and trees, here and now, immersed and baptized in moon and wind and stars, the real world, the wonderment of this life and people coming back again assuming their true roles.

Amid enormous opposition and resistance, new shoots and leaves push forth, new avenues of life, hungry for the sun, growing into cognizance of the light of the universe, trembling with resolve, willing no longer to abide intermediaries in their search for their connection to the heart and meaning of the cosmos.

It is all within. It is our quest, no one else's.

Men and women, the source and the power.

Bring forth the real gods.

FAITH

"The faith that stands on authority is not faith."

-- Ralph Waldo Emerson.

YOUR LIKENESS IN THE MIRROR

Our lives extend so far. Each ambiance of motion ripples in unseen ways throughout the fabric of time and space.

Those things we thought unimportant, simple acts or gestures, rebound throughout the halls of the cosmos and find expression in similar kind in peoples' faces, their gestures, their ways of moving about our lives.

It is impossible to fathom. One's life extends out in unfathomable ways.

The helping hand given becomes the helping hand received.

One looks into the face of one's benefactor and fails to recognize the friend one aided in Roman times.

Everything passes, yet remains, to return in unforeseen ways.

The heart is constantly making gestures.

Remember your likeness in the mirror.

HIROSHIMA

Harriet Beecher Stowe, author of "Uncle Tom's Cabin", was living on the campus of Bowdoin College in Brunswick, Maine, when she took up her pen and began writing the book that was instrumental in galvanizing public opinion on the slavery issue just prior to the Civil War.

She wrote:

"Up to this year, I have always felt that I had no particular call to meddle with this subject. But I feel now that the time has come when even a woman or a child who can speak a word for freedom and humanity is bound to speak."

And speak she did. Uncle Tom's Cabin documented in passionate and heart-rending detail the tragic breakup of black Kentucky families sold down the river to slavery. Almost overnight, the characters of Uncle Tom, Little Eva, and the villainous Simon Legree became household words. In its first year, the book sold 300,000 copies and became an international sensation.

The central theme of the book is that slavery and Christianity cannot co-exist. Mrs. Stowe saw slavery as part of a vast interlocking social system based on profit, with no regard for the human cost.

Although she was only one woman, her courage and passion stirred the moral conscience of an entire nation.

We have just passed another anniversary of the dropping of the atomic bomb on Hiroshima, on August 6, 1945. We pay homage to the memory of this event, and yet these horrific weapons of death still remain on alert in our country's arsenals. Thousands of them, each with a capacity now many times the destructive power of the Hiroshima bomb. We have already spent over a trillion dollars on the manufacture and upkeep of these weapons - weapons that are capable of totally obliterating entire cities and populations - indeed, of destroying the Earth itself.

Here in America, we hold these weapons at the ready. Given the circumstances, there is no doubt we would use them. Why else would we have them?

What would Mrs. Stowe have said about these weapons?

I think she would have said that they, too, are incompatible with Christianity, or with any other religion that advocates the sanctity of life.

To incinerate millions, or even hundreds of millions of men, women and children in the blink of an eye - to push those buttons - this is something totally incompatible with the words and intent of the founders of all the major religions.

And yet we hold them.

It stares you in the face, something appalling, yet we will not look at ourselves in the mirror.

Yet it is there. And it is spreading.

Who are we? Who are we in America?

Is this part of the Dream of America?

If Mrs. Stowe were alive at this time, maybe she would write a book to awaken us all from this nightmare.

WE ARE THE FORERUNNERS

This world, this America, will change when I change.

I begin the process. Others follow.

My path becomes the path of innumerable others, young, bright successors, moving from out the heart of the universe, down from the mountain, taking their place, seemingly insignificant and unknown, yet bearing upon themselves the tide of the future, the hope of humanity.

A religion of the future., A spirituality of the future.

Loving the animals. Respecting each person as a flower of the universe. Treasuring all, denying no one admittance to the broad circle of humanity. Racking our brains and muscles to care for all. Using our heaven sent talents to inspire others, to raise others, to bring forth and foster those mightier and more talented than ourselves. To care for nature, seeing in nature the mirror of ourselves. Giving of our hearts to others. Working for a generous, magnificent future. Selflessly pushing ourselves so that others may live and breathe more freely.

Letting flow through our thoughts and deeds undreamed-of goals and visions hearkening from the core of life itself. Believing in our own unfathomable power to fashion the new reality.

Believing in a new America. Believing we were born to create a new America. Knowing who we are.

We are the forerunners.

Here, now, and forever.

_____

FIRST AND FOREMOST

"I'm for truth, no matter who tells it. I'm for justice, no matter who it is for or against. I'm a human being, first and foremost, and as such I'm for whoever and whatever benefits humanity as a whole."

--- Malcolm X.

I AM THEM ALL

Forever here, my changeless life changes, my names fill infinite volumes, Jim, John, Emmanuel, Judy, Jane, Elizabeth, Wayne, Phil, Mary - I am them all, faces coming and going, mothers and fathers, brothers and sisters, refracting in the mirrors of the universe, clouds of galaxies of people, spumes of stars, voyages beyond number out of the darkness emerging and sinking and emerging, mighty deeds, mighty myths filling untold volumes; now the true story emerging, myself, who I am, filling the vast boundaries of the cosmos with my heart and mind, joyful beyond joyful to be alive and singing new tunes.

LET WISDOM FLOW

Let wisdom flow out upon this land.

Wisdom to fill the minds and hearts of the youth of America.

Dream dreams that go beyond anything we have imagined up until now, dreams that rock the world, upend conventional wisdom, destroy the limits of possibility.

This is the mission of America. It is a mission that has been buried in the muck and mud of nitty-gritty reality, divisions, self-centeredness, brutal politics and uncaring economics.

It is a mission that lies in our deepest collective self. It is why we are here.

To bring this out, to express things never before given expression, to create a new world, a new civilization, to go beyond what it has meant to be a human being on this planet - this is our task.

It unfolds from the simplest things. It unfolds from the heart.

It is awakening to a new myth of America - a great epic written each day by millions upon millions of simple lives, a chorus of overcoming, a rising paean to the human heart. A myth of innumerable new actors and actresses, striding forth and holding aloft a new banner of revolution and loyalty to the greatest dreams of mankind and aspiring to do nothing less than achieving them all.

We have never brought forth the great dream, because we have been shackled by darkness, by self-deception, by doubt, by hesitation, by unawareness of our inherent power. Time and time again, we have given away that power - to the despot, the charlatan, and the priest.

People are rising up all over the world, a sense of power imbuing their lives, dimly felt as yet, but stirring, stirring, spreading like a contagion from mind to mind and life to life.

This is the stirring of America.

America is spreading around the world.

Not the America of old, the military presence and machine and overwhelming might, nor the arrogant sense of a special people, the terrible arrogance and ignorance of the heart, the American flag, red white and blue and trod on you.

No, the real America is beginning to emerge, the vessel launched from the heart of all the world's peoples, a compendium of universal dreams and aspirations, voices innumerable out of all known history and out of all unknown history.

It is one person awakening. One person. One by one. Two by two. Four by four, and on and on, connecting our hearts by filaments of a new realization, new lights, the heart of humanity itself, the life of the Earth speaking now as one, as a planet birthing itself into a star.

Bring us into this realization.

Youth, follow your hearts! Create your dreams, because they are the dreams of the universe.

Come together as one now, into the unknown.

THE HEART OF SOMETHING

The light as it filters through the sky and the streets and people walking is so lovely and intense and real.

We are here, out of all space and time, walking, working somnambulistically, not at all aware of the immense importance of this moment, unaware of the astounding reality before our eyes.

Moving, breathing, yet oblivious to the heart of something. Out of all eternity, standing on this very corner, observing.

There is a life behind and within my own body extending out from my face and arms and eyes to the sun and stars themselves.

Everything around is my life.

Standing in this small, yet pivotal, corner of the universe, I am at the center. Everything moves from my own life. Everything moves in similar fashion from everyone's life, only we have not yet awakened.

———————————

FAILURE IS IMPOSSIBLE

"Failure is impossible."

> -- Susan B. Anthony.
> Civil rights leader, who fought for women's
> suffrage in the United States.

_____

THE PEOPLE TO COME

Life unfolding in immense diversity. Horses and dogs and cats and alligators and chimpanzees and birds in a whirl and the whole incredible parade of good and evil characters, villains, do-gooders, shopkeepers, business men in suits, the stars of our world, and war and peace and hatred and love, and a single soul at the heart of it all, learning, growing, manifesting, drawing upon the heart of the universe amid nuclear explosions, atomic bombs, hydrogen bombs, asteroids beaming toward the earth, this one soul expressing and manifesting it all.

These are the people to come.

They are greater than you and I, but they could never be here but for you and I and our delusions and illusions, they are going to expand upon the land of America and bless it from the farms and fields and manhattan towers to the blue rivers and majestic mountains, the sounds of America, the sounds of people marching from the infinite past, drumming their drums, playing their bugles, they are coming to announce a new world.

HERE AND NOW

Religion comes down to our behavior as a human being.

All the talk of God is garbage if a man or a woman displays the dark side of human motives and interaction.

Compassion is at the core. It is a matter of enlarging the scope of who we are, of our own core identity, and transferring that to another person.

All the talk of judgment day and armageddon, piety and faith, is all a corrupt delusion if it cannot help to create a better and more joyous day right here and now, this very day, in this world.

This America is where the dream is to be built and enacted, or it is nowhere.

There is no dream world after we die, there is no judgment day that is not judged of the simple motions of each day of our intentions and actions, and the creation of a better world before our very eyes, what we do, what we think, what we say, what motions of the heart we extend to others.

The great originators of all religions were no greater than we ourselves. They only brought to the fore that which we all possess, they tackled their demons head on, they showed the way.

No one is greater than the simple man and woman. History tries to teach otherwise, but in vain. It is all a lie.

The great Treasure Tower, arising from the heart of the Earth - bedecked in jewels, broad as half the earth, sounding with flowers and music - is our very own life itself.

We are that fabulous.

From dream worlds beyond time and space, the intent of the cosmos is given expression, the very meaning of what it means to be alive, of what this existence portends into the past, present and future.

It is your own life. You are the center of your universe. The stars are like flowers bedecking your being.

Nothing is impossible. You are irrepressible.

Give play to your dreams - especially the youth - carve them out painstakingly, inch by inch, yard by yard, never giving in. There is time of all eternity to show your face and to win.

Believe in yourself. Give expression to the power and bound-lessness of your life, which reaches the stars and nebulae.

Look into the mirror. Everything around is yourself.

Look for the jewel, it is there. It also lies in the heart of all the other people you encounter.

This is the great awakening.

It takes place, here in America.

_____

PRAISE THE SOURCE

Such praise was given out over the millennia to the beings of heaven as to fill universes of space and time.

It was never imagined to praise the source.

Myself.

_____

THE ROOTS OF AMERICA

The real roots of America are waiting to be discovered. It has nothing to do with the Founding Fathers, or Christianity, or Indians, or the pledge of allegiance, or Pilgrim Fathers.

The roots of America are found in the heart of everyone on the face of the planet.

It is an eternal home, a place where everyone can get back to and find himself or herself among friends. It is the common, unadorned human being. It is the place where you recognize yourself in all others.

America is a dream because we have not yet awakened. When we get back to our original roots, we awaken.

We see who we are.

We see who we have been all along.

147

ONE OF A KIND

Never compare yourself with others. You are one of a kind.

The universe looks upon you with a mother's fawning eye, dreaming impossible dreams through your very own mind, wanting these dreams to give shape to things never before seen.

Our task is to link our heart with billions of others, and to make their hearts our own.

_____

UNFURL THE FLAG

America is a great dream.

I sing it out from my heart. I let my voice ricochet and reverberate upon the halls of Eternity.

I stand here in the center of all time, and call it America.

Will you join me?

Come, let us roll it out.

Unfurl the flag of the true America in the wind, waving high over the land, over the hills, over towns and cities, the people, the magical people, the people of the Dream.

I will live it in my life. I will carve it out where it never was before. I will make you see.

A new breed emerges, drums rolling, cymbals clashing, shedding forth upon a darkened world flashes of hope and light.

You see them everywhere. Legions of lovers of the world.

Shopkeepers, hair stylists, insurance salesmen, mechanics, taxi drivers, lawyers, teachers, trash collectors, woodworkers, computer programmers, farmers, grocery clerks, typists, doctors, nurses, house painters, real estate brokers - the whole astonishing array, actors and actresses of eternity, living and breathing a new dream, a new myth.

Building a new meaning into the word "Democracy".

They are come. They emerge from the Earth.

_____

POWER

"We have it in our power to begin the world over again."

-- Thomas Paine.

THE UNIVERSE IS WAITING

The universe is waiting.

There will be no response, until the resolve in one's heart overcomes the doubt in one's mind.

To become everything, to overcome everything, and still more, to wrack one's brain and sinew, to have faith beyond anything.

It is all within oneself.

Dream big, and move the levers of the universe with your heart.

_____

BENEATH THE TUNDRA

The vast plains of America, the upheavals, one hundred fifty years from silent prairies to smog-choked cities and sky-scrapers and internet comradeship beaming over the entire globe.

We were never meant to repeat the same age-old patterns and cycles, the same old stories and dramas.

America was meant to be something new.

It was hardly to be imagined. The buffalo hunter crossing laboriously the frozen landscape and bloodied bodies of bison littering the ground as far as the eye could see, did he dream of a new world, did he imagine a new circumventing of the mind's eye around the globe? What was the profit? A few gold coins, whiskey a plenty, a night in the whorehouse?

This was America unremembered. This was America reduced to a lone standing tree in the cold, a wind off the Arctic, emotions as elemental as the elements themselves, brute force, anger, hunger, dumb opposition to an elemental world pressing down with brutal force. And death. Death strewn about the landscape. Unavoidable. Unanswerable. No exit to the utter constraint of cycles of sun and moon and winter, spring, summer, autumn, winter again.

This was the beginning.

Even then a miraculous world existed beneath the tundra, the frozen landscape.

It was there from forever. Whoever could grasp it, could fold it into their bosom and heart, would be free forever.

But there was no key. The wolves howling at the moon cried for a resolution. Crows perched on bare trees showed desperation in the hollowness of their eyes. It was a definite sort of madness.

This is the America crying for expression. This is the land, there is no other, it is right here and now.

———————————

COURAGE

"You gain strength, courage, and confidence by every experience in which you really stop to look fear in the face.   You must do the thing which you think you cannot do."

-- Eleanor Roosevelt

LOOKING INTO THE MIRROR

Looking into the mirror, who is there?

Eyes, nose, smile, cheeks, hair.

But something more. A self. A person. Laughter, frowning, moods shifting as light on the water.

I look you in the eye.

Shades of constant change, here and now, gone forever in a flash.

And still deeper? Who is there?

An intimation of something deeper, my being reflected in a pond, a mirror, merging deep into the heart of blackness, deep into something larger than my own beating heart, a presence, a voice, a string of unremembered words.

This is where the world turns.

This is where the light of dark suns issues forth.

It is all there in the picture of the mirror. It is myself.

It is you and I, and everywhere.

Praise be to that Self.

_____

161

THE ANIMALS ARE WAITING

The animals have been waiting.

The birds, the leopards, dogs, bees and seagulls, the elephants dancing in elephantine circles, hooting with their trunks - at long last!

America!

HOMELESS

I met a young man this evening who is homeless.

A youth who is on the verge of losing it all; talking in a tight, clipped manner, giving out nothing, holding in; non-recognition in his eyes.

He is our son and brother. He is one of the youth of America who have lost hope, who see no light, who are groping and tense and afraid, expecting any moment for a bullet to come whistling out of nowhere to end it all.

He is telling us something.

This land, with all its might, its stock markets, its precision-guided missiles, its parade of politicians looking for the next photo op, is for many a nightmare.

Standing there, frozen in motion, no options opening, a darkness consuming him, a look beams from his eye that says "What is this?".

We have brought him to this point. We are all there.

What can we do for this young man? Give him a dollar, ten dollars? Put him up for the night?

A job will not save him, nor money, nor a new car, nor a vacation in Hawaii.

He senses something, a menace to his being.

Though he may have tried, there is no place in our world for him to fit into. He is homeless.

He is the embodiment of where we all are, to a greater or lesser degree. We do not fit into this universe anymore. We have all become homeless.

Where is the dream of life and America that will nurture this young man?

We all need a new place to stay.

_____

THE PEOPLE ARE WAITING

So many people want to leave this Earth.

They yearn for a final reckoning, a dispensation of divine justice, an eternal damning of the unfaithful.

The rivers and skies and lovely meadows and animals and birds of this world mean nothing.

Rising upon clouds of a chilling beauty and foreverness they go to the land of the just and the faithful and the good and the god-loving.

Goodbye, forever, damned Earth!

These are the dreams of legions of people. They have been waiting for centuries and millennia, and still they wait.

Each generation waiting and waiting, and still the time has not come.

Meanwhile, generations live and die, are born and perish, and cycles of violence and greed and anger regurgitate upon the lands and the oceans, and fires burn in our hearts, and we yearn for an end to the suffering, a cessation of pain.

And the stars burn so brightly in the night sky, so cold, so chilling.

And so lovely.

VISION

"It is a terrible thing to see and have no vision."

"We can do anything we want to if we stick to it long enough."

"I long to accomplish a great and noble task, but it is my chief duty to accomplish small tasks as if they were great and noble."

"Life is an exciting business, and most exciting when it is lived for others."

"The best and most beautiful things in the world cannot be seen or even touched. They must be felt with the heart."

-- Helen Keller.

GALAHAD AND GUINEVERE

It is the same old drama all over again.

Sir Galahad and dragons, Guinevere and the Holy Grail.

But now the protagonist is You.

Sword in hand, to move, to break through, to believe utterly in yourself. This requires courage.

Devils swirl about, doubts careen through one's mind, determination vacillates moment by moment.

To bank your life on one more step. To face a possible abyss and to move on, one foot after another, facing possible annihilation or madness.

Everything hangs in the balance.

We can do anything. This is the secret and the reality. The universe is a giant wish-granting jewel.

Every wish is to be had; but the heart has to be tempered and shaped, like the finest steel.

Our dream pitted against utter darkness and doubt.

Can we hold out? Can we hold on?

Never bend, never waver; or wavering, rebound to the task, with increased resolve.

It is a battle fought in Eternity. It is win or lose; and winning, a gigantic portion of the universe, stars and moons and suns and even whole galaxies are swallowed and give nourishment to our mind and heart, ourselves becoming a small universe, and then on and on, devouring parallel universes, never an end, infinite growth, infinite pain and suffering and joy.

We thought we were so small. We thought time and space so small.

The secret was hidden well.

Now let us become who we really are.

_____

THE CENTER

The wind swirls demonically, a twister, a hurricane, a giant whirling dervish, trees and roots torn up, flung into the sky.

This is our world.

Debris spins off the circumference, wars, threats of wars, housing crashes, money vanishing by the trillions down sink-holes, suicide bombers, political attack ads, religious fanatics, end of the world coming, oceans polluted, AIDS and heart attacks and diabetes, fires and drought and drenching rain and tsunamis inundating whole islands, no vision, no heart, no love, no caring...

And all the while, I am at the grocery store, selecting a bundle of chard, picking over green beans, among people. They flow around me with their carts.

There is something quiet here, like the calm at the eye of the storm.

A flower can bloom and show itself here, and not even feel the wind.

This is my self. This is the center.

This is the center that needs to grow until it consumes the wind itself.

The center of the world, my heart, needs to grow.

173

OBSTACLES

Never give up on the dream. Dreams are the boat of passage to a greater self and a greater world.

Fulfillment of the dream, in the deepest sense, never comes without a deep inner change and revelation. A deepening of faith is required. To receive the dream, handed to you on a platter, without effort, without struggle, without battling doubt, without inner growth and overcoming, is no benefit at all, but rather a poisonous illusion that will lead to stagnation and suffering.

Obstacles in life are great opportunities to expand ourselves, to reach a higher state of being. Looking at them thus makes them our friends and allies.

AMERICA IS ONE PERSON

America is one person.

America is not the crowd. America is not a hundred million people.

America has never been more than one person.

That person can rule the universe, and send shockwaves of change across the plains and mountains and seashores, and loose mega-nuclear explosions of light and understanding reverberating through the bones and marrow and blood of an infinite chain of friends and ancestors and progenitors and unknown neural connections of an infinite number of cosmic galaxies reaching to the heart of everything that is or ever was or ever will be.

Your heart moves everything around you. Your heart can change the shape of the very cosmos itself, because you are the cosmos, you have that power.

Believe in yourself.

_____

SOMETHING NEW

"I have an almost complete disregard of precedent, and a faith in the possibility of something better. It irritates me to be told how things have always been done. I defy the tyranny of precedent. I go for anything new that might improve the past."

-- Clara Barton.
Organizer of the American Red Cross.

LIBERTY, AT LAST

I could feel the earth.

Rounding the curve of the road, off to the right there were cat-tle, immersed in the wet mud, and the denseness of the land-scape, the fields, the countryside, the heavy feeling of the land that was like a denseness, a feeling of being drawn inex-tricably into the heart of the landscape, mired in the mud, for-ever bound.

This was the America of the past. This was the America of my past.

To break forth from the mud, the mired-in feeling, the dense feeling of being bound by the heart to the past. Forever re-membering everything of the heart, yet breaking free now, mouthing passages of praise, of gratitude, this is my America, this is the land I have felt in my heart forever, I want to repay all debts, I want to give honor to all those coming before.

What can I say?

It is cornfields and the early light of day, and vast stretches of land. You have felt it yourself, it is in every American's blood, it was born at Shiloh and the fields of the dead, this is the mystic land, this is the land whose brothers' blood fertilized the furrows for the arising of a new land, a new life, something we had never imagined, beyond our imagination, it is come, it is America, land of my birth, land of the world's birth, we come here searching for the myth, but it is the same old story, the same repetitious stories handed down and enacted from prehistory and beyond, there was never a relief, never the dream actualized, never an end to hunger.

O say can you see, by the dawn's early light!

Liberty, at last!

Liberty from delusion, liberty from darkness, liberty from the endless migration from shade to shade.

Give me new stories!

Holding our mother's hand, we feel her heart, we are embraced, we are forever enfolded in the arms of this universe and the next, bringing forth a new world, emboldened, confident, sure of our intent.

Broad the landscape, enfolding all, a new spirit, a new vision.

Breathing life into the recalcitrant mud.   Bringing forth light from the darkened earth.

Hunger for a new world.

TURN IT TO JOY

Whatever is in front of your very face - confront it.

Turn it to joy, to overcoming.

There is nothing that cannot be surmounted.

This is the nature of life, the secret of living, all our problems and sufferings there to propel us on to a greater state of life. Never back off. Seize the difficult issues and advance, gaining light and brilliance and wisdom.

Compassion, like a flower, blooming in our very lives.

And remembrance of all things gone before, tears dropping down in deep appreciation, appreciation for these very hands and arms and eyes and lips that sing songs of praise and thanks, the utter miracle of being, the wonderment, everything made new, coming to grips with who we really are, the stars and suns in our voice, innumerable beings inhabiting the very orb of our body, urging us on, appearing at every turn, faces and dramas building to this very space and time of now and forever.

We are here, as in a dream.

We awaken.

We awaken here in America.

NEVER GIVE UP

"Just don't give up trying to do what you really want to do. Where there is love and inspiration, I don't think you can go wrong."

-- Ella Fitzgerald.

COMING HOME

America.

Dawning over misty fields...

A dream held in abeyance for aeons and aeons, now a ruddy glow on the horizon.

Birds heralding the dawn. And a cadence of drummerboys in the distance.

Then appearing, gathering on the low hills; spreading out and coming into view, an entourage of dancers and flutes, and drummers leading the way, brandishing their sticks boldly in the dawning light.

Birds and squirrels and muskrats and opossums and deer stop in their tracks, ears cocked at this extraordinary breaking of the dawn.

They come on now, singing, dancing. Their numbers broaden on the horizon.

Nameless men and women, young and old, carrying memories of all that has gone before, births and deaths, wars, tragedy and tears; now turning everything boldly to joy and laughter. It is the dawn.

America...

It is a transformation of everything.

They appear at last, from the very heart of the universe, in this mystic land.

We have seen them all before, mothers and fathers, children, sisters and brothers from an incalculable past, bearing all of the heartache and injustice and hopelessness and loss and fear and death - enduring beyond all enduring - and bringing it all to the fore now, overcoming everything.

America...

"Oh, say can you see! By the dawn's early light!"

We have waited forever.

Now they are come, heralding the great dawn of America - America, the mystic land, home of the brave, land of the free, where now they appear.

They are you and I. We are these forerunners.

We assume no august appearance.

Jack of all trades, knife sharpener, insurance salesman or saleswoman, mother, teacher, garbage collector, professor, dishwasher, pole vaulter, house painter - Buddhas of a thousand faces and names - all forged in the fires of the universe, come to this mystic land, this America, finally, to tell all over once again the great stories, and to script them with happy endings.

It is forever. It is Eternity. It is this beautiful land.

America...

We have been wandering the universe, exploring galaxies and black holes and endless lives, without ever coming home - home to ourselves, home from the myriad of identities and poses.

America is where we all come home.

****

188

ABOUT THE AUTHOR

James Hilgendorf is the author of four other books, "Life & Death: A Buddhist Perspective"; "The Great New Emerging Civilization"; "The New Superpower"; and "The Buddha and the Dream of America".

He is also a filmmaker and the producer, along with his brother John, of The Tribute Series, a highly acclaimed series of travel videos that are in homes, libraries, and schools throughout the United States, several of which have appeared on PBS and international television. The website is www.tributeseries.com

He and his wife Elizabeth have been practicing Buddhism together for forty years with the SGI, or Soka Gakkai International, a Buddhist lay organization with 13,000,000 members in 192 countries and territories around the world. The international website for the SGI is www.sgi.org. In the United States, the website is www.sgi-usa.org.

The author's books are available in both paperback and e-book format through bookstores and their online stores, online at The Tribute Series, or at Amazon.com and other online booksellers.

LIFE & DEATH: A BUDDHIST PERSPECTIVE

by James Hilgendorf

"A sensitive and profound look into the eternal
questions of life and death from a Buddhist
perspective...highly recommended."
-Midwest Book Review

"Having read all or parts of nearly a thousand
books dealing with spiritual matters, I cannot
recall another that so simply and effectively blends
the fundamentals of religion and science."
-Michael E. Tymn, Journal of Religion and
Psychical Research.

In a wide-ranging, profoundly liberating tapestry,
this book weaves together Buddhist history and
ideas, science, psychology, near-death
experience research, and personal experiences to offer
unique insights into the subject of life and death.

Reader's comments:
"A must-read!"
"A life-changing experience."
"This book has changed the way I will live
the rest of my life."

102 pages, $12.95

THE BUDDHA & THE DREAM OF AMERICA

by James Hilgendorf

"There is a revolution coming.

"And as it reveals itself in the mind of each man
and woman, the mountains will fall and shift, chasms will
open, the deserts will run with rivers, beautiful blooms will
burst from dry dust, suns will sprout in the sky,
animals and birds dance, the nuclear force of ten million
stars will break forth with light, and the minds of men and
women will reflect in every aspect of their lives
the halls and mirrors of Eternity"

"For most Americans, Buddhism conjures exotic
images of faraway lands, mysterious statues and monks
in colorful robes. But with his excellent new book,
James Hilgendorf proves Buddhism also reflects the
American experience."

-- Scott Nance
The Washington Current

149 pages, $12.95

THE NEW SUPERPOWER

by James Hilgendorf

From the book's cover:

Hiroshima. The Bomb. Madness.
The Buried Dream of America.
Quantum Physics. Buddhism.
The Individual & The Universe.
Reality. Mirrors. Delusion.
Who Are We?
Cause & Effect.
Extraordinary Ordinary People.
My Mother. My Father.
The Buddha.
Spirits of the Land. War. The Real Battle.
The Beginning & the End of Time.
The Roots of America. The Lotus Sutra.
Electrons. Karma. Hibakusha.
Fishes & Birds & Bison.
The Ceremony in the Air. Revolution.
The Intent of the Universe.
Happiness.
You and I.
The New Superpower.

It's all here in this book. Come on in.

128 pages, $12.95
Available through bookstores, or online at:
www.tributeseries.com

194

THE GREAT NEW EMERGING CIVILIZATION

by James Hilgendorf

"A new spiritual civilization beyond even age-old dreams, beyond anything we have yet imagined, is struggling to be born. It is here and now. It grows from the wreckage of despair, of lost hope, of pollution, greed, injustice, hatred and war. It is the compassionate heart of the universe itself coming to fruition and bloom."

In this book, the author describes a new world that is even now beginning to emerge - a new civilization, and a new spirituality and religion, that will eventually utterly transform all of known history and all our lives.

"At the core of this book is a plea for human dignity, just societies and a peaceful and sustainable planet - all essential if we care about the world we live in and will leave to our children and grandchildren."
--David Krieger, President
Nuclear Age Peace Foundation

"A visionary and forward-looking beacon of hope."
--Midwest Book Review

"Part memoir and part manifesto for a new world... compelling stories of his own meandering journey through life that brought him to the ideals he expresses on these pages."
--Theresa Welsh, The Seeker

184 pages, $14.95

CPSIA information can be obtained at www.ICGtesting.com
Printed in the USA
LVOW090501050312

271581LV00001B/2/P